Wolves Of North America
(Kids Edition)

Speedy Publishing LLC
40 E. Main St. #1156
Newark, DE 19711

www.speedypublishing.com

Copyright 2014
9781635011081
First Printed October 27, 2014

Wolf Facts...

Wolves are large carnivores — the largest member of the dog, or Canid, family.

Wolf Facts...

Wolves are common to all parts of the Northern Hemisphere. They are usually shy and cautious around humans but unlike the dog, have not been domesticated at all.

Wolf Facts...

The most common type of wolf is the gray wolf, or timber wolf. Adult grey wolves are 4 to 6.56 feet (120 to 200centimeters) long and weigh about 40 to 175 pounds (18 to 79 kilograms).

Wolf Facts...

Wolves hunt and travel in packs. Packs don't consist of many members, though. Usually, a pack will have only one male and female and their young. This usually means about 10 wolves per pack, though packs as large as 30 have been recorded.

Wolf Facts...

Packs have a leader, known as the alpha male. Each pack guards its territory against intruders and may even kill other wolves that are not part of their pack.

Wolf Facts...

Wolves are nocturnal and will hunt for food at night and sleep during the day. Wolves are voracious eaters. They can eat up to 20 pounds (9 kg) of food during one meal. Since they are carnivores, their meals consist of meat that they hunted.

Wolf Facts...

A wolf can run about 20 miles (32 km) per hour, and up to 40 miles (56 km) per hour when necessary, but only for a minute or two. They can "dog trot" around 5 miles (8km) per hour and can travel all day at this speed.

Wolf Facts...

The earliest drawings of wolves are in caves in southern Europe and date from 20,000 B.C.

Wolf Facts...

Wolves have friends. Wolves howl to communicate with other members of the pack. Researchers have found that they howl more to pack members that they spend the more time with.

Wolf Facts...

The Cherokee Indians
did not hunt wolves
because they believed
a slain wolves' brothers
would exact revenge.
Furthermore, if a
weapon were used to kill
a wolf, the weapon would
not work correctly again.

Wolf Facts...

Wolves do not make good guard dogs because they are naturally afraid of the unfamiliar and will hide from visitors rather than bark at them.

Wolf Facts...

Wolves have about 200 million scent cells. Humans have only about 5 million. Wolves can smell other animals more than one mile (1.6 kilometers) away.

Wolf Facts...

A male and female that mate usually stay together for life. They are devoted parents and maintain sophisticated family ties.

Wolf Facts...

Though many females in a pack are able to have pups, only a few will actually mate and bear pups. Often, only the alpha female and male will mate, which serves to produce the strongest cubs and helps limit the number of cubs the pack must care for. The other females will help raise and "babysit" the cubs.

Wolf Facts...

Wolves evolved from an ancient animal called Mesocyon, which lived approximately 35 million years ago. It was a small dog-like creature with short legs and a long body. Like the wolf, it may have lived in packs.

Wolf Facts...

Wolves can swim distances of up to 8 miles (13 kilometers) aided by small webs between their toes.

Wolf Facts...

Dire wolves (canis dirus) were prehistoric wolves that lived in North America about two million years ago. Now extinct, they hunted prey as large as woolly mammoths.

Wolf Facts...

Unlike other animals, wolves have a variety of distinctive facial expressions they use to communicate and maintain pack unity.

Wolf Facts...

Wolves were the first animals to be placed on the U.S. Endangered Species Act list in 1973.

Made in the USA
Lexington, KY
30 May 2019